Removing the Kimono

Anne M Carson is a Melbourne writer and visual artist. Her poetry has been published in both the USA and Australia, including *Best Australian Poems* (2005). She is the winner of 2011 Martha Richardson Poetry Prize and equal first-place winner in the 2011 Stones Winery Poetry Prize. Anne was Commended in the 2013 Max Harris Poetry Competition. She has curated two programmes for Radio National's PoeticA and hosted a series of poetry and music soirées, most recently the River Soirée on Herring Island which raised funds for the Melbourne River Keepers.

Anne has edited *The Sounds of Colour: Stories by Mothers of and Workers with Children on the Autism Spectrum*; *Expresso Chapbook*; *Choices from the Heart: A Collection of Stories*; and *Kaleidoscope: Stories about Autism through the eyes of Mothers*.

She teaches poetry to adults, is a trained social worker, and also works as a creative writing therapist. Her visual art is based on photography and botanical specimens. Her photographs and art panels have been exhibited in galleries and florist shops and used as greeting cards, bookmark and literary journal cover.

www.annemcarson.com

For Helen and

for Ian who believed it would happen

Ian Gordon Murray 25/8/42–12/7/12

Removing the Kimono

Anne M Carson

HYBRID
PUBLISHERS

Published by Hybrid Publishers

Melbourne Victoria Australia

© Anne M Carson 2013

This publication is copyright. Apart from any use
as permitted under the Copyright Act 1968, no part may be
reproduced by any process without prior written permission from
the publisher. Requests and inquiries concerning reproduction
should be addressed to the Publisher, Hybrid Publishers,
PO Box 52, Ormond 3204.
www.hybridpublishers.optusnet.com.au

First published 2013

This printing 2014

National Library of Australia Cataloguing-in-Publication entry

Author: Carson, Anne M, author.

Title: Removing the kimono / Anne M Carson.

ISBN: 9781925000245 (paperback)

Subjects: Australian poetry.

Dewey Number: A821.4

Kimono image: Tayler'd Creations
Cover design: Jo Marchese

Table of Contents

Prologue

II

III

Epilogue

Prologue

*The only worthwhile joy is to release some infinitesimal
quantity of the absolute, to free one
fragment of being, forever.*

Teilhard de Chardin

Notes

---

kiri   Also known as Sapphire Tree, Emerald Tree, Imperial Tree,
            Foxglove tree: *Paulownia tomentosa*. The tree has its origins
            in China and is also known in Japan from ancient times. It is
            named after the daughter of the Russian Tzar, the Queen of the
            Netherlands – Anna Pavlovna.

shoji   Sliding ricepaper doors

Oba-san   Aunt (respectful)

tansu   A chest, chest of drawers or cupboard

obi   Wide and long pieces of fabric, often of a contrasting colour and
            design, used to secure kimono at waist

koto   A Japanese zither about six feet long, with thirteen silk strings
            passed over small movable bridges

The *Kiri* tree and the girl
Paulownia tomentosa

My father planted the *kiri** the day I was born; both of us growing green and sap-filled. By the time of my first steps I already looked up to her – my other true self. I grew straight, solid, father said, for all my willowy grace. When my secrets needed an open ear it was always to her I turned. In spring her blossom fragrance wafted through the *shoji** – vanilla and almond – perfuming the whole house. When upset, I would place my palm on one of her heart-shaped velvet leaves, calmed by its hugeness, her steadiness. *Oba-san**, my dance teacher, said I had growing to do to become as big-hearted as she.

Father would cut her down when I married; a master wood-worker would turn her into my wedding-*tansu**. Childhood was shaped by that looming loss – a hard knot in my heart. How to make my life worthy of her ... Opening the *tansu*-door for the first time opened my eyes to real beauty – honey-coloured timber shone, each join exquisitely crafted, all eloquent with her presence, absence. I had to harden myself against tears. The loss and gain have been a twisted heart-vine ever since. I had a special kimono made from silk dyed the exact shade of her lavender, had the hem decorated in prints of her blooms, the *obi**-brocade embroidered in emerald.

When she lay in pieces in our garden I collected her twigs – so many lie in bundles in the kitchen-*tansu*, drying. I'll have them treated – a lifetime's worth of eyebrow pencils – when I perform she'll be with me. There is wood enough to have a *koto** crafted from her timber. When I coax a song from it I know it will be her voice reverberating.

I

*Won't you come and see
loneliness? Just one leaf
from the kiri tree.*

Bashō

Corvid

A colloquium of crows crowd into the valley.
Hundreds fill the floodplain – the only venue
big enough to host them. Some gather
in the old pines, forty-foot-tall pavilions.
Below, ewes and wethers shelter, sheep-coats
the same calico colour as the bleached branches.
The congress lasts for days. We don't know
what they discuss but they start early.
A wall of sound reaches us on the salt-fresh air:
harsh, rudimentary articulations shredding
the dawn silence. Mid-morning and dozens
line the fence down the Sand Road, pepper the hill
with black blotches. The atmosphere is charged
with concentration. At the last minute they notice
our approach, rise with one mind, one wing;
a dark seam wrinkling the air. They fall
like a jagged breath, back to earth. A diva
in batwing sleeves flings herself into an updraught,
towards another bird in tails. They fly into
each other, shoulders glancing, a caution-thrown
-to-the-wind dance, practising a savage ballet.

Heron ministers to the morning

Yarra River, Victoria

At first glance everything seems
in order; water covers the tree's
toes, laps the bank, thigh-high.

Pied cormorants roost on dead
boughs, ply their way upstream
and down, family groups together.

Water reflects stretches of sky,
wind-flecked fragments of khaki.
We mosey along, play delicious

hooky from daily life. The lull
of water laps the hollow metal
hull, the engine idles on a theme

of its own making. From his pulpit,
a heron ministers to the morning,
dove-grey coat, delicate manners,

so softly spoken the wind takes
his words, whisks them into ether.
We cannot hear his warnings, his

caution about eels – is there water
enough for migration? If the adults
don't venture north, no elvers will

return to the Yarra ... He leaves it
hanging, stands a moment in silence,
shoulders hunched, one leg crooked.

Self-portrait
Dampier Peninsula, WA

Something drops away from the iris, the lips,
tightness melts from the cleft between the eyes.

Days of bird-watching make my face like theirs:
emptied of the habit of self-consciousness.

No bird is impressed by what I wear, by who I think I am.
You can pour out the self you imagine real in the world

like you pour your body into the brine-warm rockpool.
Let light invade the body, the way the sun shines

through ruby panels in the black cockatoo's red
tail feathers – stained-glass brilliant against the sky.

Morning lazes in the shallows ...

Brahminy Kite, Dampier Peninsular, WA

Morning lazes in the shallows, stretches
towards noon with the tide. The sun wheels

its barrow of embers across the sky.
On the headland Brahminy stakes out the tallest gum.

Sentry at the checkpoint on land's end; chestnut chaps
with feathered jodhpurs, crisp white jacket.

Nothing escapes the scan of his minesweeping eye.
A whimbrel in camouflage colours enters his airspace.

The kite's warning ripples across the splendour
of the bay. Silence bulges but does not burst

nor does the whimbrel falter – his wings maintain
their grasp, dipping in and out, air-oars

shipping his body south. Later, Brahminy lifts
from the branch clean into air on hunger's mission,

a russet scarf disappearing into blue;
painting a perfect miniature on sky's clear canvas.

The rain of bodies

Glenaire, Victoria

Pods of gang-gangs hurl sleek grey bodies
into a receptive sky. They surf, rising and dipping,
catching air-current waves in rows from ridge

to ridge. Red-capped males lead. Querulous calls
resound across the valley. The empty space above
fills, opens out – a book I've always wanted to read.

Down the road, duck-hunters in camouflage gear
camp by the jetty, waiting for the season to open.
I dread dawn's mayhem, the broken plumage.

Early morning, the *pop pop* of distant guns interrupts
sleep, innocent as a child's replica, doing its deal
of damage. No peaceful transition from sleep, no

dream tatters curled about the mind to mull over
while the billy boils for breakfast. All I think of
is the rain of bodies, the thud as they hit earth.

The birds engrave circles

Crested Terns, Balnarring, Victoria

The birds engrave circles above a flickering school
in the shallows. Wings find purchase in air as if it's solid
ice they push against. Feathers bite like blades. They wheel,

perfect speed-skaters bunching and dispersing, circling
in tandem, hitching a moment's respite from another's
slipstream. They jostle like lads, shouldering for vantage,

for the hell of it, courting collision in almost-contact sport.
Speed is prized, so is poise. Spills are few. They plough the sky,
wings back-leaning, as if flight were an artform still visible after

the birds have gone. They're masters of water, handsome
in naval white, black crests like skipper's caps at jaunty angles.
They study the sea for the flick and wriggle beneath. One

movement, fluid as thought, on a plumbline to beauty. Snap!
Wings shut on impact like fans. All beak; a long yellow skewer,
rising with its glistening prize; a shining slither dripping light.

The crucible

Jacksons Road, St Andrews, Victoria
for NN

I

The main house used to nestle in its green nook – the forest
thick on three sides busy with untold life. Now I drive

through the eeriness of a silent waiting army, uncertain
if it's in retreat or advance. Each individual trunk,

black as soot. There is nowhere to hide. When I reach
the place where the house once loomed, the concrete slab

is all, no height to flesh out space. The buildings
have been scissored out of the frame, snipped clean away.

The fringe of garden has gone – the Himalayan rambling rose
over the arbour you'd cut bracts from for my table or yours,

the Nellie Neal graft in the bed by the kitchen – all gone.
All the fire debris is gone. I can't bear to enter your space

without a door to step through, without the privacy of cupboards
to protect your things. I walk the slab's perimeter,

mourning the artworks, a studio full – yours, friends', colleagues',
valuable and cherished. Your treasured pieces of jewellery,

a life's worth of belongings, vaporised in an instant …
but you and the dog, mercifully saved.

II

Further down the drive the vegie patch with its sagging
jerrybuilt chicken-wire fence is gone. The enormous black wattle

that lit up like a candle each season is burnt to a charcoal crisp.
I can hardly bring myself to turn the final corner.

I slow my car to a crawl past where the tennis court stood –
the ruts still tipping me from side to side – hearing the echo of games

played in spite of the shonky net …

III

I park where I always parked, walk over, enter from the front –
my shoulder remembering the task the stuck door

always asked of it – though there is no doorway, no timber,
no handle … nothing to help me handle remembering …

… absolutely nothing left.

IV

All the hand-hewn, knobbly timbers have gone.
The hand-made mudbricks; I loved them

as if it was my thumbprint which marked them, my palm
which had shaped them. I gave up everything to live between

the pale ochre-rendered walls which once held hope over me.
I staked my future on growing into an artist here. For seven years,

I stoked the creative fire, heaped up coals in the hearth.
The house heated; an alembic, bubbling with chemistry.

Each night I lay down pulling dreams and fears towards me,
holding them close the night long. The unceilinged roof

let the dust and debris of the universe in, let in the numinous night
and its minions. Insects favoured the mudbrick for nesting,

the chinks for egress. Frogs hopped under the dresser,
an echidna into the water-bowl I left out for birds.

In the light of ecumenical candles, witnessed by foraging rodents,
my longing took the long journey of translation into practice

of the craft, the work. Other self-sufficiencies followed;
swinging a decent axe, stacking a sturdy woodpile.

I returned to the city, newmade, leaving the mudbrick cottage
to its fate.

V

I had been gone six years the day the bush erupted.
The vineyard went wild as wind sucked the fire onward

and flames vacuumed up the valley. The cottage would have
been first, a vessel heated past endurance. Cacophony, explosion,

nothing left whole in its wake. They rescued you, defending
a circle of precarious safety around you in a maelstrom.

VI

I turn, close the door on that time. My longing is long gone
from here. Before I take the curved drive home, I photograph

new leaves, magenta sprigs bursting out of the skin of the old,
the burnt. It will never be the same but it will become

forest – home again to creatures. Nature has such flagrant
disregard for stasis. I hoist my swag of memories, walk away.

Spending time with Desiderata cows

Glenaire, Victoria

I'm greeted by cows' curiosity, doleful eyes, long-lashed blinks.
Facing me at the fenceline, their bodies run east to west. *You can't*
fool me, I tell them, *I know how smart you are. You read ley lines*

with your bodies, line up on the earth's latitude. What's stopping you
now? The cows look dumb; ponderous, patient, Desiderata cows.
I remember the research: Google Earth showed cattle all over the globe

orient north/south but powerlines confuse them, stop them aligning.
Here, overhead, wires sway in graceful arcs. *There's the culprits.*
I pitch bush camp in a secluded spot. In the distance aged pines

spread across the floodplain, refuge offered under their limbs.
I set out on a daylong walk. The cattle have aligned north/south
at the far edge of the paddock. *Clever fellas, aren't you?* I tell them

on passing. Late in the day, the fenceline leads me back to camp.
Bellowed pain announces the herd. A ragged line at the milking
shed, strung out like ebony beads on a necklace. They remonstrate

with the absent farmer. Their anguish, the bulge and swing of udders,
ushers evening in. Night becomes custodian of silence but for
the metronomic hoots of owls and the scurrying of rodents in leaf litter.

Later, the ragged breath and fierce gutturals of creatures mating.
At dawn, shrike-thrush song greets the day. The cows are clustered
higgledy-piggledy on the sodden field. Grass is emerald after rain,

the herd brilliant black in contrast. I prepare to leave. The cows
gather to watch me ferry gear back to my car, my visit an event
in their lives. Setting sun is bright on their curious, patient faces.

Death by Mozart

Dampier Peninsula, WA

Back to Broome on the tangerine-dirt highway after five bush days,
tripping on surreal colours, space, birdsong.

Does the world still exist? Ahead a black pall announces something dire –
a strange, troubling beauty; pewter on kingfisher blue.

Colours all-of-a-piece, harmonious despite the almost-blacks of danger,
greys of foreboding. Are the billows cloud or smoke?

We close the windows, joke about shades of Armageddon – slate, charcoal,
the crimson of fire and blood; all the doom-laden hues.

If I'm going into oblivion I want to be listening to Mozart,

the driver says. He puts on a disc, blasts us with glory.
accelerating through the leaden haze. We expect a furnace,

trees shedding cloaks of flame, metal-melting heat. Instead –
fire-spikes, grass high, scamper like lizards, lick the red dirt at the road's edge

salamanders, not dragons, behind this belch of doomsday smoke.
No need then of the *Requiem*, just yet.

Suburban cricket

Dad's got the tranny and Richie Benaud calls the shots.
Ball-leather dinks on wood, sixes thwack and a smattering

of applause fills lazy Sundays with restrained strains
of Britannica; English as elevenses, proper as pikelets.

The clip of mum's secateurs, the scratch of dad hauling
branches accompany catches, congratulations, the patter

of cricket commentary. They work the garden, I work my tan.
Sunbaking is such an aural act. Whether it's WACA or Gabba,

words are pitched for the nursery; googlies, dibbly dobblies,
dollies. Players hoik balls, tonk them, hook sixes and fours.

They nurdle balls out of reach, mullygrub 'em along the ground.
Inside players' flannels are their silly legs – white, knobbly

like dad's, lanky from his togs. They say *groin injuries, jock
straps*, without snickering. Masculinity tucked out of sight

in trousers baggy enough to hide the bulge in the bodyline
but for the *look-at-me* red smear on out-of-bounds body parts.

Dream in double-0 gauge

My father's dream in the wooden fold-down box
is huge and bolted to the wall. Release the catch,

unfold the dream. A world in miniature, articulated
on sturdy trestle legs. Smells are dusty sharp –

the nasal smart of methylated spirits. Throw the switch
and life comes to Tiny Town. The engine crosses fields

of tufted grass, rolls through level crossings. Herds of placid
plastic cows graze mountains with stuck-on fluff for snow.

Home has warmth; a wife, children and a dog who waits
and wags. The good life lights up windows, bids him

welcome. This man – homunculus – is the apple
of my father's eye. He packs his briefcase full of dreams,

takes the daily carriage, workward. The evening steam-train
wings him home. The motor in the engine has copper

filament coiled tight as boyhood hopes. Silver tracks gleam
in the pocket of the night, the train-set in the magic dark.

The air holds its breath

Life swirls around us. Our guests mill
in the vestibule, spill onto the footpath,

sharing grief and reminiscence. No-one notices
the hearse pull out from the kerb, the lead man's

measured pace. The air holds its breath –
an undercurrent shivers out like an eddy

stirring just a handful of leaves. It brushes
my mind, prickling. My sister notices too.

The sky like a lid on a box, lowers. Underfoot,
the bluestone is hard. Death has us in a press.

We turn in slow synchronicity, each sealed
in her own sling of sorrow. Time opens,

draws us into a pocket of pain and departure.
We watch the hearse move away with our father's

unaccompanied body. Around us, inside us,
molecules rearrange, adjust to his dying.

Leavings

Descending in the lift we speculate about love letters, secrets,
joke about windfall and contraband. My siblings and I, beneficiaries,

approach a foot-thick metal door, just like in the movies.
Somewhere between jail and an exclusive hotel (sealed lips,

mum's the word). Behind the door – our father's safe-deposit box,
contents now to be revealed. A uniformed, holstered guard greets
us,

her face a mask of discretion. Suddenly serious, we pretend
nothing can shock us. We show the key, she marks our numbers

on a clipboard, waves us through. We turn to watch her leave
the room, like a butler, gliding on castored feet, paid not to notice.

The key is poised. Will it be like peering inside my father's
underwear drawer? My brother opens the box. Discarded on one
shelf,

crumpled bands from wads of US notes, but only a few crisp singles
remain, high-denomination, fresh from the mint. Scribbled memos

about where he spent it – casinos, trips abroad, dollars for
one or two friends. We take a while to twig: it's just the wrappers,

the leavings tucked away, outside the tax-man's ken.
Reminds me of a possum's nest revealed after pruning

(intricate snug in a thicket: stubs of two carrots, ancient apple core).
Inside my father's nest – mere remnants of his secret hoard.

In therapy with Fred Williams

Red is for pain, ochre for earth in the painting over the mantel
in the therapist's room. I glance again and again.

It pulls attention, even composure – a coloured counterpoint
to my life in words. The huge black slash of bushfire-burnt log

felled on the painting's forest floor. It's a body-shaped
cigar, almost smoking. Against other trees it's a colossus.

Is there always a dead body in therapy?

What my father stirred in me hangs over therapy like the painting
over the mantel, the canopy over the forest. Like the man over

the family. Only this time he's forced to silence, forced to hang
back while another talks. He has gone, fallen down, man to earth;

a dead colossus in the forest. By the time I finish, the smoke
has stopped coming out of him and he's no longer too hot to handle.

Against the downward pull of death

Gariwerd (the Grampians), Victoria

I

The rock is adamantine grey, curved and coloured
like animal hide. We're fleas scaling a beast's flank,
hauling our sacks of dead weight against the downward
pull of death. Just a twitch would fling us to the stony floor.

II

Lichens stain the rock with sluiced greens, pale pinks,
blues – pastel patinas. Even in hard places, fertility is various
and kind. Filigreed petals unfurl into papery rosettes.
Emerald mosses, tenacious in adversity, asking little.

III

Clefts and pleats show where rock was riven then folded
concertina-fashion. Cliffs plunge and rear. Sandstone boulders
have been scooped and scoured by winds over aeons of
weather. Rockfaces are shirred, smocked by seamstress time.

IV

The comfort of huge and solid matter – obdurate life on a vast
scale. Against threescore and ten, the finitude of all things
human, this is geologic time, glacial movement. We touch
rock, reassured by unarguable fact, effortless endurance.

II

*Come! See
real flowers
of this painful world.*

Bashō

Spooning under the Milky Way

Croajingalong National Park, Victoria

Your warmth presses my back,
sand's cold reassurance beneath.

Restless wind tosses its questions.
A shawl of stars drapes the shoulders

of the sky. High overhead pinprick lights
mesmerise the dark. Held in a pod

of pleasure and pain, poised
in the whirling night, the two of us

present to the immensities, patient
while they do their work, honing

the human, so we too become vast,
and all that is paltry in us, blown away.

Your eyes are deep grey lakes in the sky

Darebin Creek, Victoria

Springtime has ramped up tones a notch past lime;
I show you lush lemony tips of new growth –
                    chartreuse grasses.

My way of introducing you to my photographer's eye,
my predilection for colour. All the cones are happy,
                    humming.

Your eyes are deep, dark-grey lakes in the sky.
Hydrological eyes, weather
                    watching.

You notice flood-wrack hanging in rags from the boughs,
Pilbara, I say, *the Aboriginal name. Only* they *have*
                    the exact word.

I hardly know you, but enough to know you like words and water.
You catch my eye; mirror-neurons fire
                    bridging difference.

So much light, the scene is awash. The shade-dappled creek
is transparent in patches; I can see straight
                    to the riverbed

and its collection of boulders, its pebbly floor. In other places
water reflects foliage, the lemon-lime light
                    of connection.

The seduction of shaving

Long and soft like weed under water,
your beard is winter-white but for dark patches

at mouth-corners where your youth pokes through.
I comb with fingers, tugging handfuls to make playful

emphatic points. Our first morning-after, my fingers
map the planes of your face, learning your body

all over again. Fragrant with lovemaking, I don
a black silk dressing-gown embroidered with magenta lilies.

You are placid under my blade-wielding hand.
Barbering is so erotic, tender. You bristle at my suggestion

that you hide behind your face hair. *Natural*, you say.
But shaved you show more: camber, nuance of expression,

lips' twitch and pucker. You ask, *Is there evolutionary gain?*
We agree that beards protect but just who benefits is not so clear.

*

In the high country bushfire tree-skeletons stubble
the mountainsides like patterns of beard growth. I clip

your whiskers with nail scissors from the first-aid kit.
When I finish we're sprinkled with a confetti of hairs,

the romance of snowfall out of season. Now, after 38 years
you decide to shave it all off, bare yourself like a white cedar,

showing its structure of bone. We find a razor shop,
together. Your diffidence dizzies me, shifts perception;

you could be the son I never had, I'm taking him to buy
his first razor. This moment might be all the son I'm

allowed. A whole life pressed into the space it takes
to choose Philips from Ronson. While you shave

grizzle from your face, I photograph your reflection
in the mirror, another thing I might have done for a child,

celebrating a pause on the path to adulthood. But –
no son of mine will ever be, nor will a son of ours.

The flash from the camera seems like an illumination,
a blessing. I wash short, tough hairs from the vanity,

watch them spin down the drain. In bed I run fingers
over smooth skin, kiss the man, unhindered.

The sound of absence

Air particles shift in waves through walls
and space, towards me, the air displaced

by your car, plowing a path through traffic.
Next door a woman's heels knock on floor-

boards. I feel it in my body, not noise but
vibration. The blade of absence hones me.

With closed eyes, feet up, I wait. Fern-frond
shadows drift across my lids, a watch on a

chain, taking me deeper, deeper. I turn
aural. Sounds become equi-valent; rich,

intricately textured. The fridge's groans and
shudders no less pleasing than the liquid

melody of the magpie or the whistle of wind
in the elm. Underneath sound, stillness so

alive it thrums. Things utter themselves
into silence.

It's hard not to be biblical.
The listening ear, the singing world.

I take up a long, lone branch, bone-white
Wambelong Creek, Warrumbungle National Park, NSW

I lie balanced on the beam of a flood-felled tree,
a bridge from bank to bank. Like a hand at my waist,

a branch keeps me from falling. Water tumbles over
pebbles after storm with liquid ease, flowing

unencumbered. The river's cool breath rises.
I hear the hollow *thunk* of pebbles' percussion

as you prise them from the riverbed, toss them aside.
The sounds connect us in silent camaraderie.

I take up a long, lone branch; bone-white, water smooth,
ballast as I place foot after precarious foot,

as if over Niagara. The grip of shoe rubber is palpable
reassurance. Halfway over is hardest – a bird in the cage

of my chest scurries – the stream's not deep but I fear falling.
Balance is an act of faith. Will taking risks here teach me

other trusts; in myself, you, the wide, worrying world?
Upstream, you make happy industry, damming

and undamming water, aiming to turn what is multiple
and dispersed into singular and strong. The mess

of rivulets and runnels is tidied into one deep channel –
a curve of grace you carve in the land. You revel in the power

to change the river's course. What is excavated, what runs free?
The stream surges like a horse given its head. It tolerates

handiwork as readily as boulders, branches, floods. You know
it will shrug you off at the first chance, as lightly as leaves.

Play is ephemeral, mysterious.

While I learn to balance on my beam, you practise malleability,
turn your hand to the beauty of the running stream.

Songs of the mysterious river

Houseboat on the Hawkesbury River, NSW

We wake to water thick as mercury. The sky hoards light
behind gunmetal clouds. Not foil's brilliance but the blunt polish

of tin dumbing day down. Rock cliffs hold the pressure in;
disagreement broods over the boat and roosts like a bird of prey

in the dinghy all night. Oyster shells exposed in the ebb tide
shine jaggedly, open-mouthed. Something's got to give; fifteen

impenetrable fathoms. At last a lick of wind breaks the impasse,
light's small change, coins and medallions as far as we can see.

A belated sun finds expression. Now the river is as profligate
with light as you with endearments; the more brightness, the better.

So much reflection – each pale piece mirrors
a corner of sky, a mosaic of metals overlapping.

*

At Staircase Bay crows bestow their crooked blessings, whipbirds
lash the morning. A colony of crickets berates the heat.

Sound arrives in waves, rocking silence. Trees perch on the lip
of the escarpment, toeholds in shale, subsisting on dirt and minerals.

Sun favours the foliage of salmon gums. On the ridge, a lace
of trees inclines to sky. Elsewhere aubergine, mandarin, mushroom-

toned rocks. The relief of human insignificance starts a slow burn
of exaltation. I relax into emptiness, dark and splendid joy.

*

We climb Gentleman's Halt. You decline to rest at the halfway rock,
leap ahead sure-footed. I sit in a cicada circle. A solo starts

to my right, soft, singular. Others spark up, an orchestral net
of sound spirals around me. The volume rises, falls, a tidal pulse

synonymous with summer. You join me; now we bathe in sound.

*

The tide turns and jellyfish return on their silent migration.
Ghostly moonfaces drift in and out of view; uncanny creatures,

a foot across, tall as toddlers. Multiple tentacles trail behind,
floppy as the limbs of knitted toys. Two together, batches

of singles; hundreds in a bloom, tumbleweeds
in a watery prairie. They pulse, filter water through transparent

gills like mushroom flutes. At the mercy of currents,
they venture the river, then out to sea again.

*

We coast to a sandy bay. I let wet rusty chain-links play out
and the anchor bites. The boat swings round the mooring

with loose abandon like a child about a pole. We open blinds,
windows; lie in the narrow bed. The night seeps in with scents

from the mysterious river, songs of lap and swell. Stars are broken
mirror flecks flung onto velvet; the boat rocks, cradles us to sleep.

Jiving with Buddy Holly

I slide in the CD and you melt back into boneless adolescence,
long lolloping limbs folding into the front passenger seat.

I watch the music suck you bodily into the ethos of the song,
the era of the beat. Your head folds forward into nonchalance,

a private hunch between raised shoulders, a secret
self. Your body comes alive, a coiled spring of beautiful

male energy held loosely under compression. You tap the beat,
eager to escape the trap of the suburban bourgeois. If you

had a mop of hair, hanks would flop over your forehead,
your eyes – a curtain drawn for privacy.

                                I wind down the window,
feel the 60s blowing through us, potent as fuel.

The car purrs like an EH Holden. If I looked down I'd see
bobbysox with sneakers, tapered pants, pert breasts

in a pointy bra. I imagine you calling me your *girl, baby.*
You're loose enough now to jive, rubber enough for rock 'n' roll.

Turning tawny
Warrumbungle National Park, NSW

We pad the campsite perimeter,
night prowling until we settle and curl
in our nest over dew-damp, flattened grass,

just a wisp of tent tarp between us
and the starlit sky above.
The great rock's presence blesses us,

asking nothing, giving shelter
with its flank. Orion beckons then dips
below the horizon. Kangaroos

are gone to their night camp, emus too,
picking paths with their dainty toes,
their shapely leather legs.

You turn tawny in moonlight. I greet
your pelt with my hands, making
its acquaintance. I flex and soften under

your heavenly body.
Our love startles birds on their roost.
We belong to the night

lent to each other for safekeeping.
Answer to a long-held question,
you still night's hungers, day's demands.

To a flame

The long day has passed – supine at last.
We turn to each other. No need for candles

to set the mood, to show the way. We know
each other by heart, by Braille – all the raised

and hollowed contours, invite touch, tongue.
You wave off a moth that joins us in the dark,

drawn to our flame. It returns, circles our faces,
as if they shone with light. The wings' soft

whirr brushes our skin like hands bestowing
blessings. I stop pushing it away, accept its being

in the bed with us, its delicate caress on cheek,
chest, the blunt butt of its head. We dance

our slow dance – boundaries deliciously blurred,
grateful for the gifts of the gracious night.

Before diagnosis

Mallacoota Inlet, Victoria

My hand is to the tiller – the motor chops water into clods.
They catch the light in a fanfare of phosphorescence
before collapsing back into blade-turned foam.

Ploughed furrows fan out behind in a widening V.
An escort of crested terns fly wide reconnaissance circles
mistaking us for fishers, waiting for handouts.

They keep careful company before one dives, glimpsing
the glisten below, a wriggle of life loosed from the clods:
garfish, sprat, worm of the sea. I turn for home.

West is to starboard, home of the sun, stage for the daily
death of light. We are not headed there tonight –
but you never know when you may need the ferryman.

The harbour is our destination, through the deep river,
into a dusk prodigious with light. Silver slicks the water;
a glory line of beaten metal ascending to sun and sky.

Could dying be like this, stepping into the numinous?
I cast a mindnet out into the world, trawling sky, earth,
water for poems – nourishment for a hungry mind.

Partaking of the other

The clerk called it a 'shortening', you say. We're heading home,
cosy in the car's cabin. Dusk creeps up, blurs boundaries
between day and night. For a while each partakes of the other.

The bird of uncertainty hovers, shadow more pronounced than
usual.
You wouldn't know from our banter. *Shortening, that's a baking
term
isn't it?* you ask. *Yeah, you put it in pastry to make it short.*

Your confusion reaches me in the dark. *Butter, oil, too,* I say.
*Imagine a spectrum – at one end bread, damper. Dough with stretch,
give, draw it out long and lean on the workbench. Add more butter,*

*rub it in to make scones, a pat more for pie crust, even more makes
biscuits. Then right at the end is shortbread – delicious, so full
of butter it crumbles in your hand. You can't get shorter than that.*

You listen intently – I've never seen you so interested in cooking.
Silence falls easily. We dwell on the shortening which took you in
to Births, Deaths and Marriages. The exemption we needed

from the month-and-a-day notice to marry – granted only if it's dire.

Probably fatal, the doctor had written. *They waived the fee,* you say,
voice lifting with wonder at the small, kind human gesture.
We let it resonate – a temple bell sounding the deepening dark.

Transubstantiation

Lake Frome, SA

It feels like the edge of the world. We've been flying
for hours, in metal as flimsy as foil. Three of us
squashed into proximity, strangely solitary

in cocoons of raucous silence. The engine whine
is constant, bone-juddering. Our disembodied voices
crackle with headphone distortion, keeping talk

to a minimum. Wind rushes my legs from a hole
in the fuselage, arctic cold, the outside brought
inexorably in. The seatbelt and discomfort

pin us to the present moment, forcing what is
essential to the fore. Flying over Lake Frome,
on our Lake Eyre honeymoon; I never imagined it

like this. The lake stretches to the horizon, mostly dried
to salt, liquid in places, like an enormous Miró canvas:
long languid brushstrokes, vivid pleasing shapes.

They seem intentional, chosen for balance, juxtaposition.
Below us are two finely etched scimitar curves
of sand, the larger poised over the smaller;

warm cocoa and ivory against light lapis; harmonious,
muted colours whose like I've never seen. The further
we go the less substance. The parallel is not lost

on me; already your cheekbones foretell your fate.
We fly into thin cloud cover with the same lacy texture
as the saltpan, the same bridal white.

Horizon disappears; now we're *inside* a Miró –
shape, line, light made three-dimensional.
I swallow vertigo at being so unanchored,

bereft of the usual safe parameters. The landscape
mirrors our predicament perfectly, extreme
and beautiful at once. There is no choice but to proceed.

It's a gallery of light performing variations on a theme –
radiance, luminosity, incandescence. The space
opens into something grand, dazzling and terrible

with the capacity to take everything. Instead of falling
off the world, we're in danger of melting into it,
leaving all expectation of substance, certainty,

continuance behind. We are the only solid matter
amongst the ephemera of salt and cloud.
All the shadows have been swallowed, pure

aesthetics remain; pristine, solitary splendour
existing mostly outside human ken.
I hold what is most precious up to that presence:

my wedding vows, the kind of companion
I hope to be to you, come your end. Let them be
transfused by that simple illuminating truth.

Compression

I

I lie on the camp-bed in your room, accepting your fate as well
as I'm able. You can see why they called it *passion* – it will take

all the life-force you have left in your still-beating, existential
heart. You're on the bed nearby, just an arm's reach away.

More auditory than physical – only the smallest stitch
holds breath to your body, bellows breath, rhythmic in its own

drawn-out mechanical way. Almost gone, just a wisp of you
keeping me company as I keep company with the dark.

Despite hospital corners, disinfectant, here is a wildly tender place
to be. Only the outcome is known in advance – not the manner

or measure or means. You're making a kind of music I think
I recognise. I strain hard to hear the beauty of the melody,

a tune you taught me, so dear I have it by heart. But it's gone,
only the sostenuto of the *beat, beat, beat* remains – like the soft

blurred burr of rhythm sticks.

II

On the other side of my bed, a cold metallic chill seeps through
the glass. It's from the moon looking down, casting her glance

our way. It's not that she doesn't care but her care is for the order
of things – she tends to endings as well as beginnings, is impatient

when we lose track of the circularity of that fact. She'd have us
mindful and deeper. It's not personal – I read blessing when a ray

of her light slants through the curtains across your brow. When I
can't bear another rasp from your throat I find comfort in her counsel.

III

The animals do it so well – at home in the world, snug under cover
of darkness. When their time comes – no complaint, only a foetal
curl,

a sigh, letting it come as it will. Your philosophy, too, letting
the wildness come as it will, uninterfered-with by you. Just now

a raucous blooded howl of protest outside our window shatters
the precarious peace – an animal, prey to the irresistible other, like
you.

IV

I lie, a petal pressed between the pages of two thick volumes –
on one side of me you, busy with your final chapter – on the other

tales told by the mysterious night. If I'm to be pressed between
two volumes of wild writing will I emerge with my colour

no less intense but made fast, my words compressed? Strength
is not the point, it's having heart enough to let you go.

Maybe heart and how it works its symphonies is all it was ever
about. Like the petals, I'll turn transparent – light shining through.

On the ebb-tide

Shelley Beach, WA

I leave people behind, beaches ago, share the arc between
the long curved arms of the bay with oystercatchers, a couple
of storm petrels. The sky is a long way off – aerial benevolence
bestowing space, calm. The landscape has me

in its loose hold. I haven't forgotten sorrow. It's a relief
to wear it on my sleeve, not keep it tucked in a back pocket
for later. My throat opens like a gull's; grief thrown
to the wind, tears into sand. The birds don't mind,

nor does the sun, which shines or not regardless. Ahead on the sand
I see a metallic shimmer. Up close, movement, life – a large
beached fish, sand caking its coat like crumbs. Beached hard
in the sand, it gasps dreadful heaves, body-long.

I imagine it's ailing, is perhaps old when the great impartial hand
of water hurls it at the shore. Minutes I gaze into its bright
wide-open eye not knowing if I'm looking at wisdom or vacancy
but knowing that life looks back.

I am not long from *your* struggle to the death. Accompanying you
to the threshold and having to let you go has calibrated me to dying.
Nights listening to your gasp, learning to let the ebb-tide reverse
a lifetime's bond with healing.

Now I don't know if the fish is trying to live or trying to die. Perhaps
I bring death here from your sickbed, impose my slant on the scene.
Maybe the fish is not ailing, just took a wrong turn at the rocks,
a ghastly misjudgement,

sucked into a vortex of turbulence that left it stranded.
Do fish have moments of inattention like me? Will it die
in my presence? Large pauses open between each juddering
desperate breath. I must at least try to save it.

I try scooping it between two chalky cuttlefish bones, not wanting
to touch slime, the possibility of poison, wanting to put it in the way
of waves, a chance to swim away. The fish eye's iris flares, registering
touch. We have the rudiments of communication

but I can't distinguish flinch from breath. The wobble of the body
stops me before I even lift it from its bed in the sand. There's nothing
but to overcome squeamishness. I pick the slick cold body up
in two hands, walk it out past the rocks

where it foundered. It lies still in my hands, a kind of trust, lets me
loose it into deep water. Immediately it's under the break,
disappearing
beyond the reach of my eyes – a shimmer of sleek silver radiance –
into the bluegreen eminence that is ocean.

Homage

Grok: verb (grokked, grokking).
To understand a thing so thoroughly you merge with it.
From the Martian, 'to drink'.

I notice the book poking out from under the shelf –
garish cobalt-blue sky, lurid cover-image of Mike the man
from Mars, naked and buff in water up to his highly defined
abs. Water-Brother Jill holds out beseeching hands.

Before you got sick we would read to each other in bed –
poems, short stories, longer works too, believing
we had time to practise accents, inflection.

Then words carried you beyond the reach of pain.
We paused for hospital visits halfway through *Stranger*
in a Strange Land, skipping the bad bits – '60s sexist kitsch,
rants, ribald humour, intrigued by Heinlein's iconoclasm,
his inventiveness. He minted *grok* – an ugly, hard, rock-like
word – but it was you who broke it open for me to the gold.

Perhaps, hidden under the bookcase, the book has not
yet heard you've gone past the reach of words.
                    If I don't move it, maybe I won't disturb
the small scrap of life-force hidden between the pages,
wedged in the thumb-eared corners, the cracked spine
precariously held in place by yellowing tape,
the pencilled annotations in your minuscule hand.

The dresser removes *The Kimono of Mourning*

I kneel on *tatami** and close my eyes.
A gust of cool air tells me
      the ricepaper screen has opened.

Orange blossom fragrance enters
with the dresser. Her feet in cotton *tabi**
      shoosh as she slips behind me,

unties the *obi**. Yards of brocade fall
about me. I feel small, vulnerable as a girl
      just presented. Arms outstretched

she holds the *kimono** seam at each shoulder,
slides fabric over my skin, silk sibilant.
      *Torihada** rises.

I wear only *koshimaki** and underrobe, light
enough now to lift from *tatami* – a kite
      loosed from its tether.

The robe is folded as prescribed, sleeve
over body, whole in half, half again.
      Wrapped in linen paper,

placed in the lacquered box. I will not miss
the silk, dark as midnight, though it had
      a touch of grandeur.

The dresser's hand and arm ripple around me.
I recall the movements in my mind's theatre –
      remember our rehearsals.

Back and forth, her hands are tireless,
eddying like wind over rice fields.
    She is to empty

me of grief. A dark spirit emerges – long
as *obi*. She is a *noh** dancer drawing
    from my ears, mouth, nostrils

the colours of sorrow. A final red, arterial scarf
from the belly, drawn out, dissolving in ether.
    She has removed

the inner and the outer garments of
my bereavement. Unmade, I prepare to start
    over, alone on *tatami*.

Notes

Tatami	Woven floor mat
Tabi	Cotton, tight fitting socks with side buttons
Obi	Wide and long pieces of fabric, often of a contrasting colour and design, used to secure kimono at waist
Kimono	Traditional Japanese garment for men and women
Torihada	Goosebumps
Koshimaki	Piece of cloth wrapped around hips
Noh dancing	Ritualised Japanese dance/drama concerned with the timeless concerns of the human condition.

A lesson in …

I near the elbow of river where I'll scatter your ashes.
All I can do is release you, trickle you into the tree-fringed
flow, let the water in its wisdom carry you away, let you
sink, white and ethereal, to the pebble floor.

                                      … letting go

III

The temple bell stops
but the sound keeps coming
out of the flowers

Bashō

Trusting the eloquence of seeds

Wilsons Promontory, Victoria

Cloaked in convalescence, the landscape without foliage
resonates with loss. Once forest, now individual trunks stand out,
painted the black of cinder and mourning. I know the theory –
bush regenerates after fire, birds return, growth rises from ash.

But the burn here is heartbreaking – hillside after hillside
is stubbled with matchstick thinness. In some places recovery
is obvious. Eucalypts have put on sleeves – pressure-bandages
on burns. Elsewhere a moss poultice covers the earth.

No regrowth yet in the banksia forests – sounds are broken and
brittle;
seedpods stay silent. Their mouths will open eventually, articulate
with seed. I will trust seeds' eloquence, their tumble into the waiting
ashbed – earth's imagination. Green is the colour when the
regeneration-

wheel turns. Shoots will appear, new ideas nosing their way into
life.
Already the grass-trees thrive. From burnt beginnings, solid spears
rear into space, fields of lingams insisting on existence. I want
to be told it again and again, until I have it by heart.

A body you cherish

Eucalyptus pauciflora (Snow Gums), Mt Hotham, Victoria

In the high country tree-bark masquerades
as metal. Trunks are kitted out, gleaming
in daylight with a show of toughness

that might survive anything. As night closes
its lid, air turns crimson. Trees turn into torches
lighting the way to a foundry at the summit

of the mountain where armour is forged.
Dawn lifts the metal-bark garment
and we see beneath to pale skin, vulnerable

to wounding. It is a body you cherish, all the planes
pleasing. Wind and rain have rounded the contours,
caressing skin's hollows. In the next valley, fire

has taken whole hillsides; to the horizon
white skeletons and stubble. The lean of the trees,
like a pattern of beard growth, shows how the wind

cut swathes. Fire flared across ravines,
up the gullies, over the razorback ridges, searing
the skin of the land, leaving only bones.

On giving away your old red scarf

i.m. Lindsay D'Arth, 1955–81

The elegance of our dance – like brolgas courting – on earth
and in air too – from body to spirit, spirit back to body –

our dance was what I loved about us most. Riding
on your motorcycle, slipping earth's tether, moving

to gravity's secret hinge. Our flirt with weightlessness;
two immortals swinging between heaven and earth.

You fell into torment the way we'd fallen into love –
without warning, bodily – losing your sky-blue nerve,

your way of resistance to gravity's pull, falling
like a stone from the sky, flat on your back on forest's floor.

A new centre of gravity in me;
the core fragile, easily shattered, the cast of each day grave

as a cemetery, full of the dark birds of death,
circling, whirling, very near, closing in on carrion.

Your death was the bundle I lugged like weighted animal skin
through the years' tundra, eating dirt and rock.

Gravity teaches humility, patience, lays down gravitas
like an open misère, but who wants lessons such as these?

Two decades until I become as gravid with words
as a womb, as a comb of bees.

Your scarf – from the rug shop in Marrakesh – used to be red
as cyclamen, vivid as blood – faded now to palest rust.

*

The cemetery engraves a threadbare hill, parched paddocks,
bleached grass. I knew you'd been cremated

but the smallness of the mound … just big enough to rest
the plaque on, the ashes under. The absence of a grave,

of a body-shaped mound shouts *gone* into the dismal air,
shocks me into grief all over again.

Styx

I toss and turn, wear a body-shaped groove in the bed,
the way your body made dog-shaped beds in the ground.
I don't want this day – which has you in it – to end,

nor the morning to come or the hours that follow
to follow. If you were Mongolian we'd bury you deep
in sky, laid on earth not under, a blanket of clouds for cover,

on a mountain close to the gods, wind's whistle for company.
We'd fold your tail under your head, and pray
it would transform to a human ponytail next time round,

though I don't know how your life could be bettered.
On the byre we put bracts of banksia rose, wisteria, Schmackos
to pay the ferryman. At the last minute we toss on a tennis ball,

for the person in the afterlife you'll pester for games.
That's what gets us smiling again, the tennis-ball afterthought –
how neatly it says everything there is to say about you.

Emergency in the night

From the overpass, freeway cars blur
into night. Their tail-lights are a stream
of red specks racing east to morning,
like a flash of cigarette sparks caught

by a gust, reminding me of the acrid
lungful you can't believe feels so good.
Four years and I crave one now; the taste,
the bloodstream rush, a bolt of courage,
borrowed toughness.

                   Going home
with the empty cat cage, still seeing
his fear-filled eyes, the catch at the end
of each fought-for breath. All I can inhale
is helplessness; one of the immutables.

The detective's chair,

threadbare, stained with old Guinness, splashes of double malt.
Rebus sits into the early hours pooled in moonlight, neon,
dappled with despair, ensconced in smelly, smoky fug.
He looks unseeing over night-time Edinburgh, shoos ghosts
back into the past, ignores conflict with the brass, other cops,
even manages to bypass self-recrimination, regret, that
quagmire of his multiple failings. He comes to the centre
of concern, the current case. He may not be quite sober but
the blur is better. You can't bludgeon hunches out of hiding,
have to be willing to hang out in their vicinity, hope they
show their heads. He sinks another inch or two of whisky,
the better to see into the shadows, last the night through.
He nods off, as usual, the LP crackling as it spins, still
seeking the glimmer of clues nestled between hard facts.

Erlendur comes home after a brittle day. Nothing has broken
open in the case of the murdered boy, no motive, weapon
not even a maybe suspect to pin their hopes upon. His chair
sits by the window, blond wood waiting to welcome him.
He leaves the light off, sinks into low-slung, leather-
upholstered ease, letting his mind loose from its leash. He
offers his tired thoughts, his despair to the open sky. They
dissolve in its infinite space. His ghosts visit him – unsettling
spectres from the past. He sighs, allows them their due. Gone
midnight, Reykjavík. He always means to get up, go to bed,
but dawn often finds him curled into the contours of the chair,
cold, cramped. He goes over the facts one more time, teases
them apart to see what can be glimpsed through the cracks.

Wallander jerks awake, heart jumping. He's on the sofa again
grabbing a few hours, still surrounded by dirty laundry. Not time
enough this case for a leisurely chair by the window, letting
patterns emerge, even Puccini is relegated to a back seat.
This time it's a serial killer. He snatches thinking-space
between developments on a bleached bench at Malmö Harbour,
Copenhagen smudged in haze across the Sound. Or shut-eyed,
slumped on vinyl in his Volvo at the Ystad crime scene. Even
flat on his back in a locked conference room, desperate for
a few motionless moments to let his thoughts roam unfettered.
A niggle, just out of reach, an uneasy ache he knows holds
vital clues. Something someone said or didn't say; elusive
since the first murder. If only he could sit and listen long
enough for it to unfurl, it could crack the case wide open.

Post-industrial chic

Sydney Biennale, Cockatoo Island, NSW

The lower mandibles from five giant earthmovers
line up on the foreshore, biting on air.

An abandoned crane frames a steely cube of harbour.
Gantries and derricks, shipbuilding paraphernalia

scattered for effect. Overhead, postcard-blue
backdrops the ochres and reds of rust. Dust settles,

is swept away. What was industry is now gallery,
a post-industrial chic. The vogue is for distress;

timbers and metals, rust's flake and scratch,
its insatiable hungers. The limits of paint are plain:

muted notes on a theme of corrosion.
Dull black on pale magenta, faded '50s red and green.

We thought industry would last forever, progress
would never end yet even metals defer to time.

Here, exhibited for tourists to wonder at,
the relics of industry – a latter-day version of ruins.

A Murder of Crows

A Sydney Biennale installation by Janet Cardiff and Georges Bures Miller

The installation is half-a-warehouse huge, kitted out in timber:
gouged floors, two-foot-square pillars holding up the roof.

Wood's once-alive presence lingers. I approach a repose
of chairs, spiralling out into space, like an ear. Some hold audio

speakers on their laps, others are empty, waiting. The feel
is sparse, austere. I choose the inner circle; count one hundred

sound boxes around me, some on stands, others on wooden
planks up in the gods. There's a bank of amps off to the side:

serious sound. A horn, bell-mouthed, rests on a deal table
in the middle. It broadcasts a woman's voice

recounting nightmare: … *a house I'd forgotten I owned.*
Garden furniture almost covered in sand-drifts.

Inside the bedroom, under covers lies a severed leg still
wearing sneaker, sock. I try to scream… A single violin

takes up the tale, sings its heartbreak song. Other strings
join in, morph into the solo oboe's cry. It's high fidelity,

each speaker a single voice, pitched real. The sounds encircle,
squeeze me into the eternal long-lasting present moment.

Poignancy turns to toil, labour, the doing-it-hard heave
of Volga boatmen. Footsteps emerge from momentary silence,

so real I turn to see who has arrived. They move from speaker
to speaker, pass behind me, exit through a non-existent

squeaky door. The woman's voice resumes; *In my dream
there's a factory, running red. It's blood from cats they feed*

*into a machine. They push them in, then push in babies
and the blood runs.* Wind stirs and soughs in the rafters.

The great gaping wound of grief rises, gathers strength.
Katabatic winds hurl so loud it's physical, pummelling maelstroms

into me. I am helpless in endurance. The pain dies down,
piano lifts a chiffon of sound through the sobbing space.

Broken, rising

I sit in the café, ear open on the world.
Two Vietnamese women at the next table
talk intensely, six-toned voices rising and falling,

breaking with humour, heart. Tongues dip
into diphthongs, trip over triphthongs, lithe dance
of a language. I understand nothing but in sounds

I see story: *the rise of rice from the paddy,*
shoots the colour of trust. Grains of rain fall,
shaken from the rain-giver's basket. Rice broken

into bowls, taken into mouths. Bullets from a sky
innocent of malevolence, propaganda from
politicians' mouths. War falls – bracelet of barbed

wire around the wrist, necklace
of landmines around the throat. I see breaks
in limbs, bones pushing through flesh,

jagged rips in the fabric. Ideals break – stones
on ungiving ground. Seasons turn. Green hope
springs up in the paddy, grains of grief from the eyes.

The hard shell of tyranny breaks open,
husks fall away. The fever of hatred falls.
Bowls of broken rice shared with family, friends.

In the café, the women rise from the table,
prepare to leave. Their voices trail after them –
streamers of friendship the colour of trust.

Vietnamese is a tonal language with six principal tones –
mid-level, low-falling, high-rising, low-falling-rising,
high-rising-broken and low-falling broken.

The limits of good-will

In Berlin, pretty Berlin, in the spring time,
You are never not wondering how
It happened … Robert Haas

Post-midnight arrival on the Prague night train,
too cash-strapped to waste money on a half-night hotel.

We find a doss-house – a first – not backpacker's
but beds for the chronic homeless. The dorm vibrates

with the snores of both men and women. Huddled
in the bathroom for a final cigarette, perched on the brim

of the hand basin, we take in courage with illicit nicotine,
exhale fear through louvred windows, into the German

Nacht like so many before us. My heart still hammers
from the disturbance on the train. Czech transport *policie*

pricked Prague's romance, primed me for Berlin.
Suspicious of backpackers, unescorted women,

they rifle our rucksacks. One prises the lid off my Kodak
canister, sniffs, says *Ach!* Fires staccato Czech questions

at me. I try to convince, Vegemite is not hash resin.
Vegemite für Frühstück, I say, wanting them to share

the joke, *am der Brot.* But schoolgirl German and
humour are lost on them. My fingers mime breakfast,

a knife scraping spread onto my other hand. I'm an
Aussie backpacker, open, wholesome as a slice of bread.

I smile the smile of someone who doesn't know how bad
it can get. They do not smile back. The leader plants

himself opposite me, interrogation stance. A briefcase
on a short strap is slung from his short neck, over his barrel

chest. His colleague flicks the cabin-light switch, plunging us
into instant darkness. In perfect accord, the leader snaps

the clasp of the case, the drop-down lid opens towards me.
A spotlight inside blasts a beam so bright I gasp, shield

my eyes. He barks commands, demands papers, passport.
I'm too shocked to see slapstick; the light pins me to the seat,

rakes my eyes for fear, for Capitalist lies. I'm already cast
as drug smuggler. The third soldier keeps touching his firearm

like some men touch their balls, for reassurance, not knowing
when he'll need a charge. The encounter sears my system,

an imprint I carry to the doss-house, under the *Kapitan*'s
stern gaze, past creepy eyes, into my basic bed. Too cold

and distrustful to undress, I twist myself into knots under two
thin blankets, all my clothes, inside a narrow sleeping sheet.

All night people shift phlegm up and down windpipes. *This is
nothing,* I tell myself, *don't you dare complain.*

The propinquity of the past

Friends on a terrace, convivial coffee, crimson stains
in wine glasses. I talk of travel to France, Lisieux in Brittany

where a saint died, lurid keepsakes in booths along the way,
statues with eyes that light up when the switch is thrown,

as if this makes the miracles more real. It gets a laugh.
I describe venturing down a side alley, coming across remnants

of the war-torn landscape forty years on: sandstone walls
without roofs or glass panes, pockmarks at chest level.

Across the decades there is the echo of bullets, the after-image
of falling people, billowing a requiem of dust.

The new city, I say, is really just a skin, a sheath over
the abyss. I halt mid-word, foolish, disconcerted.

This was a dream I had in Lisieux, not what I saw there.

The walls' anguish called out to me only in dream,
where they awaited their folk as only dumb matter can.

Through the membrane hanging like a curtain between
the mind's rooms, a dream stole into the one marked *memory*.

Twice bereaved
for HMC

The first time round, it was the body
of our marriage – poor bruised corpse –
I put under and covered. I dug into

the compost leaking tears and fury. You
were as good as dead. But there were
no small solaces, like choosing the coffin

or knowing your favourite flowers in case
an undertaker asked. I couldn't write
public notices: beloved or sadly missed.

There was no ceremony to orchestrate
grief, no music or pallbearers to accompany
me as I walked away from life with you.

This time your body is for others to bury.

I'm told they took a hanger with your suit,
dressed as well in death as I'd once kept you
during life. There'll be a service

and a minister will give blessings for
the bereaved, not meant for me. I won't
wear black or carry sodden handkerchiefs.

But all the buried strife and smoulder is
resurrected momentarily with your dying.
Twice bereaved by you and never once
                    your widow.

Hanging

*In 1967 Ronald Ryan was the last person
hanged in Australia*

While we wait for the hangman
my grandmother squashes me
against her body, into her single bed

spread with widowwick.
She switches the wireless on
and we wait for Ryan's death.

A radio voice talks us through
his last hours as if there's nothing
to be ashamed of.

It drops into the milk of my belly.
I register everything, take notes
for the rest of my life.

So this is what they do,
grown-ups I mean,
this is what they're like

out there in the world.
I'm pressed between the bulk
of my grandmother

and what's about to happen.
She knows it will scare me
to meet death for the first time

up close in her bedroom:
allows it anyway. Her body
tells a secret excitement –

breath hot on my nape,
her hold tight,
hands trembling – how vehemently

my mother would disapprove.
Grandmother tries to cosy me,
but her big spoon-woman body

stifles my small-girl spoon.
She's too close, clings as if 11 years
could protect her 68.

The way my grandmother speaks
debones the deed: *putting him*
to death she says, a gentle notion,

for putting babies to bed
not the force needed to snap bone,
break a grown man's neck.

While we wait for the hangman
she tells me that the heart
is not strong enough to pump blood

uphill – you can't sleep on your left side,
the heart could just stop, burst,
its innards splattered

like a plum thrown on hard ground.
You could die – alone in the night
and never know.

I figure I'll help the heart,
never sleep on my back either.
It's my own death I learn

to fear
in the bed of my grandmother
while Ryan steps up to his.

A surfeit of lampreys

i.m. Joyce Lee, 1913–2007

I read a poem aloud to her; *a surfeit of blueness,* I say
pronouncing it *sirfeet,* a word I've never said out loud before.
Sirfit she corrects me, softening the end like a fall on snow.

The first time I heard that word was in History when I was 6.
The teacher was talking about Kings – John, I think, and how he
died.
A curious fact to make you remember history, only I never did,

I only remembered what he died from. She pauses for breath …
A surfeit of lampreys! It still delights her; she guffaws.
Say it again, Joyce – a surfeit of what? A surfeit of lampreys,

she responds, stressing *lampreys.* It doesn't help much –
I've never heard of them. *Lampreys?* I ask, introducing the word
to my mouth. *What the heck are they?* Both of us laugh now –

at the funny words, the weird death, the strange ways
to teach history; at what stays, wings folded in a quiet corner
of your mind, for 88 years. *Seafood,* she says, *some sort of seafood.*

We laugh so much Rosie the budgie squawks in her cage,
swings from the wire by her beak.
I go to the kitchen for tea, Joyce to her study to find *lampreys*

in the dictionary. *They're eels,* she shouts, *lampreys are eels!*
He died of a surfeit of eels!
So oily, she says distastefully. *And so long!* I reply.

Barricaded heart

The Federal Hotel, Kuala Lumpur, Malaysia

Jaded by city grime, clamour, tales of machete-wielding,
acid-throwing thieves, I arrive at the marble hotel entrance.
Flanked by two concrete dragons – a posse of doormen, bell hops,
maitre d', Malays in national dress. Head down I push through

the gauntlet, alert for men on the make angling for tips.
My room sits at the end of a long corridor – no aloneness
like the aloneness of a large hotel. Carpet is frayed at the threshold,
half a century to lose its nap, collect splotches: stains and smells,

ash, tobacco, vague foot and body odours, unnameable fluids.
A catch at the back of my throat scents mildew, the damp
underfoot, mould. Marble bathrooms, long-vacant ballrooms –
the hotel had a heyday. Poolside bars once a hub, now the cabana

yawns to the elements. Lift signs still boast *Shopping Arcade* –
only two still operate. The 28th floor revolving restaurant
is suffering its age. The mechanism jolts every quarter-turn,
creaking its need for maintenance, forcing a shipboard gait.

Dim, trying for atmosphere, sophistication, the space echoes
with emptiness; 200 seats, tonight just me and two others.
Revealed in instalments, a wedge at a time, KL is made beautiful
by neon, night: the soft blanket that darkness throws over grime.

The spell lasts half a revolution. My eyes adjust to the dark,
drift to un-antimicassared couch-arms, oily headrests, another
tatty carpet. The mechanism jolts again as the ratchet slips
another cog. We jerk in concert, marionettes spilling haphazard

food and wine onto the hapless carpet.

                              The next time I walk down
the marble steps, brave the hotel entrance mêlée, a doorman
catches my reluctant eye. I notice the beauty of his gold brocade
sarong, his bearing. He stands-to when I return his glance, half

bows a Muslim greeting. He touches right palm to heart,
eyes intent, gentle, never leaving mine. I'm shocked at the power
of the gesture, allow what is offered into my barricaded heart.
What had become shrivelled relaxes its grip, unfurls.

Digitalis

I peel purple and lilac gloves one by one
from the stem, the pale cuffs darkly pigmented,

a trail of dots running into the depths like footprints
you can't help following. I slide a finger

into the soft dark shaft; the tapered tip, napped
like suede or fur, one for each finger. My paws glide,

tread-softened, stealthy as shadow. Shapeshifter;
one foot in the ordinary world, the other in wilderness.

Am I the fox stalking night, or the woman,
flower bells dressing each finger?

I went out once more before bed …

… the temperature had risen, a sign that we could expect snow. During the night it blew and raged. Rain pelted the tin roof, then hail, and just before dawn, the soft blanket of a brief snowfall. I dressed and walked out into a landscape beyond the reach of cliché. Each snow-frosted tree was decorated with hundreds of swinging egg-shaped pendants: storm-made chandeliers hanging against an ermine sky. They bent the branches low. Early sun-shafts glinted on glassy surfaces. The eggs bumped each other, chinked and chimed in a vast cathedral silence. The delicate crystal tinkle carried far out over the peaks.

I went from tree to tree cupping the crystal eggs, one by one between my blood-warm hands. Inside each, under layers of packed ice, a fresh, fragrant eucalypt leaf.

The lovely wild

The bats are flying home, dots in the sky
a skein several suburbs long
trailing a dark thread

against patches of bruised cumulus.
They pass overhead in silence.
I hear wind moving whiskers

on mouse-shaped faces, the murmur
of wings as they slip through a sky
softening as if fond of them

letting them pass. A breeze falls
on my upturned face;
I inhale the lovely wild.

Epilogue

When the soul lies down in that grass
the world is too full to talk about.

Rumi

Oyster of the soul

Balnarring Beach, Victoria
for JMD

I arrive the evening before to darkness so complete it ripples
like drapery around me. When I wander beachward, the sand
underfoot offers welcome slippage. At the tideline – a creature
sucks and gasps, startling me out of reverie. Breath-held moments
pass before I realise that the sounds belong to ever-hungry waves
intent on devouring the shore. In bed, night holds me safe
in its shell. Come the dawn, day bursts through the cracks, yolk-
golden. The blue-skied morning has only trust to talk about –
wide open, as the bay. The breeze tatters pollen from the wattles,
petals from the tea-trees along the drive. They catch the light
in showers of tiny sparks, spotted muslin falling to pattern the
ground.
A delicate fabric draped over rough gravel, like the beauty
and grit between us, beauty and grit working together to turn
to pearl in the oyster of the soul. There's salt on the air, floral notes
beneath, the perennial allure of blossoms. I listen, longing
for the crunch of tyre-tread on gravel, announcing you.

Acknowledgements

I would like to thank the editors of the following journals and anthologies for publishing a number of poems from this collection, sometimes in different versions:

Australian Love Poems 2013, (Inkerman and Blunt), Blue Dog, Blue Giraffe, Earth Song Journal, Eureka Street, Famous Reporter, foam:e, Going Down Swinging, Harvest, Imagine, Island, Journal of Psychological Medicine, Mascara Literary Review, Metabolism (Australian Poetry Ltd Members Anthology), Page Seventeen, Poetrix, Poetry Monash, Rabbit, Reflecting on Melbourne (Poetica Christi Press), Sketch, Sotto, Verandah, Victorian Association of Family Therapists Newsletter, Visible Ink, Windmills, and *Yellow Moon. Antipodes Magazine (USA),* and *Pennsylvania Review (USA).* 'The dresser removes the Kimono of Mourning' was translated into Japanese and published in *Red Leaves* (English-Language/Japanese Bilingual Literary Journal). 'The rain of bodies' was included in The Disappearing App by *The Red Room Company.*

'Songs of the mysterious river' (previously named 'Hawkesbury Houseboat') was awarded first place in the 2011 Martha Richardson Poetry Prize; and 'The seduction of shaving' was awarded equal first in the 2011 Stones Winery Poetry Prize. 'Transubstantiation' was commended in the 2013 Max Harris Poetry Prize. Some poems in this collection have also been shortlisted or commended in the following poetry competitions: Reason Brisbane Poetry Prize, Shoalhaven Poetry Prize, Eastern Libraries Poetry Competition, Place and Experience Poetry Competition, Inverawe Nature Writing Prize, Page Seventeen Poetry Competition, ABC Radio 360 City Nights Competition, and Yellow Moon Poetry Competition.

My deep thanks go to the many valued and generous literary friends who have offered friendship and helped shape me as a poet. Many have given specific, unstinting feedback on particular poems and others on the whole manuscript: Susan Fealy, Bob Morrow, Alice White, Alison Elliott, Helen Carson, Sue Lockwood and the Io Writers' Group, Christina MacCallum and the former Kew Poetry Group, Jenny Compton and her Carrum Writing Group and particular thanks to Diane Fahey. Special warm thanks to Jennifer Harrison and Alex Skovron for generous and insightful mentoring, to Jean-Marc Dupré for design assistance and the author photograph and to Jo Marchese for another elegant cover design. I'd also like to extend particular thanks to Anna Blay and Louis de Vries who have, through Hybrid, published this book – with superb attention to detail and in the spirit of collaboration.

Printed in the USA
CPSIA information can be obtained
at www.ICGtesting.com
LVHW022100040624
782270LV00001B/181